LIVING WITH
DIABETES

ABDO
Publishing Company

LIVING WITH DIABETES

by MK Ehrman

Content Consultant
Dawn Davis, MD, PhD, Assistant Professor, Department of
Medicine–Division of Endocrinology, University of Wisconsin

LIVING WITH HEALTH CHALLENGES

CREDITS

Published by ABDO Publishing Company, PO Box 398166, Minneapolis, MN 55439. Copyright © 2012 by Abdo Consulting Group, Inc. International copyrights reserved in all countries. No part of this book may be reproduced in any form without written permission from the publisher. The Essential Library™ is a trademark and logo of ABDO Publishing Company.

Printed in the United States of America,
North Mankato, Minnesota
102011
012012

 THIS BOOK CONTAINS AT LEAST 10% RECYCLED MATERIALS.

Editor: Holly Saari
Copy Editor: Karen Latchana Kenney
Series design and cover production: Becky Daum
Interior production: Kazuko Collins

Library of Congress Cataloging-in-Publication Data
Ehrman, M. K.
  Living with diabetes / by M.K. Ehrman.
      p. cm. -- (Living with health challenges)
  Includes bibliographical references.
  ISBN 978-1-61783-126-3
  1. Diabetes--Juvenile literature. I. Title.
  RC660.5.E37 2012
  616.4'62--dc23
                                      2011033154

TABLE OF CONTENTS

EXPERT ADVICE

As an endocrinologist, I'm a physician who specializes in treating diseases related to hormone production, such as diabetes, which is due to problems with the hormone insulin. I take care of many patients with both type 1 and type 2 diabetes. I also do research involving the underlying causes of diabetes and possible new approaches to therapies.

The teenage years can be a challenging time for patients with diabetes since they are starting to have more control over the choices they are making and the management of their diabetes. It is important for them to establish good relationships with their care providers and their families and friends. These people can help teen patients make healthy decisions and learn how to effectively manage their diabetes independently. I have a few other key pieces of advice for young people with diabetes:

Daily Diligence. Unfortunately, with type 1 diabetes you cannot take a "holiday" from your diabetes. It is important to take your insulin and manage your diabetes every day.

Control Now for Long-Term Health. Maintaining good control of your diabetes at this stage of life is very important in preventing long-term complications.

Enjoy Your Life! Your diabetes does not have to interfere with your ability to have fun and participate in all kinds of activities.

The treatment of diabetes has advanced at an incredible rate over the past few decades and people with diabetes now have many more treatment options. Thousands of people are researching diabetes every day to find new ways to improve the lives of diabetes patients. You can expect to live a long, healthy life if you manage your diabetes appropriately.

—*Dawn Davis, MD, PhD, Assistant Professor, Department of Medicine–Division of Endocrinology, University of Wisconsin*

WHAT'S GOING ON WITH ME? DEFINING DIABETES

T he thirst gripped Oscar sometime toward the end of his algebra class and the only math Oscar could concentrate on was counting the minutes and seconds until the end of the period. When the bell rang, he dashed out the room and pressed his face into

One symptom of diabetes is being really thirsty all the time.

the water fountain. While it was normal for him to take a few sips between classes, this time Oscar couldn't seem to suck down the water fast enough.

This didn't make any sense. It was autumn and not very hot. Oscar hadn't played basketball that day. He realized this had happened yesterday as well. And as he quickly dashed into the boy's bathroom, he realized he'd been peeing a lot also.

Not just that, but he was hungrier too. His parents had warned him not to eat anything heavy on the way home from school because it would ruin his appetite for dinner, but he couldn't help himself and had a burger. By the time he got home, he was hungry again.

"Oscar, are you feeling okay?" his mother asked him. For all his eating and drinking, Oscar felt weak and tired. He excused himself to use the bathroom and when he returned, his mother asked him whether he wasn't going more often than usual. Oscar was a little embarrassed talking about it with his mom, but he admitted that it was true.

After a night interrupted by frequent trips to the bathroom, Oscar woke up feeling worse than before. Instead of taking him to school, Oscar's mom drove him straight to the medical clinic.

After a few tests, the doctor came back with the news.

"Well," the doctor said. "I'm afraid you won't be going back to school just yet. Do you know what diabetes is?"

WHAT IS DIABETES?

Tests confirmed Oscar has type 1 diabetes. But, what exactly is diabetes and what is happening inside Oscar's body? Type 1 diabetes is an autoimmune disease. This means that your immune system—the part of your body that's in charge of fighting off disease—is actually causing the disease. In type 1 diabetes, instead of attacking a virus that gives you the flu or another infection, the immune system becomes confused and destroys your body's islet beta cells. These cells are in the pancreas and produce the hormone insulin. Insulin is a hormone that changes the glucose in blood into energy.

ISLET BETA CELLS— OUR INSULIN FACTORIES

Beta cells are located in strange-sounding regions of your pancreas called islets of Langerhans. Your pancreas has many of these clusters (approximately 1–2 million!), each containing a few hundred to a few thousand cells. They are able to sense when there is glucose available and create insulin in response, which is then secreted into the blood.

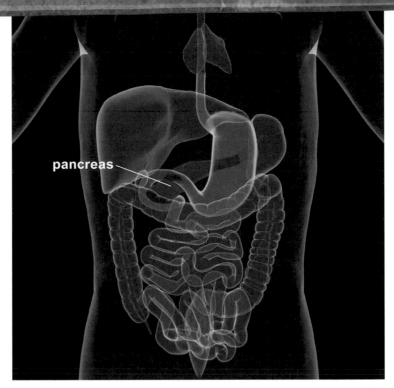

pancreas

Diabetes begins in the pancreas, the organ that produces insulin.

When the islet beta cells are gone, the body can no longer produce insulin, which means it can no longer regulate your blood sugar. Without insulin, your cells cannot take in the sugar necessary to keep them going. And sugar—or more precisely, glucose, a specific type of sugar—is the "gas" that keeps your cells running. When your cells are starved for glucose, your body reacts by signaling hunger, but even if you eat more, the glucose doesn't go into your cells where it could be used to generate energy. In fact, you're probably going to lose weight as your body breaks down fats and protein in an effort to provide fuel for the cells. The sugars that cannot be absorbed into your cells back up in your bloodstream and your body uses all the water it can get to "rinse it clean." It tries to dilute the glucose in your bloodstream and rid your body of it through urine. That's why Oscar was so thirsty and had to go to the bathroom so often. The lack of necessary energy can make you more tired than you normally would be, even though you might be eating more than normal.

Type 2 is another type of diabetes. Although it's more common than type 1, type 2 diabetes tends to affect older people, which is why it's also sometimes known as adult-onset diabetes. In type 2 diabetes, the pancreas *can* make insulin; however, it either does not make enough or the body doesn't know how to use the insulin

THE PANCREAS, INSULIN, AND YOU

The pancreas produces all types of digestive enzymes and hormones. One of the most important of these is insulin. Whenever you eat carbohydrates, the food is converted into glucose. Your cells need the glucose to do their work. Unfortunately, every cell has a membrane, and without help, the glucose cannot enter the cell. That's where insulin comes in.

Your pancreas's job is to monitor your blood sugar level. As carbohydrates convert into glucose and blood sugar rises, the pancreas secretes insulin. By attaching itself to your cells, insulin allows the glucose to pass into the cell where it can be turned into energy. Otherwise, the sugar piles up in your blood and your body never receives the energy it needs.

Type 1 diabetes can affect normal kids and teens of healthy body weights.

once it is released. While type 2 diabetes also has a genetic component that makes a person more likely to develop the disease, it is more closely connected to lifestyle—particularly obesity—and therefore it is mostly preventable. Because of the obesity epidemic among today's youth, type 2 is being diagnosed more and more often in younger patients. In the United States, approximately 3,700 young people under the age of 20 are now diagnosed with type 2 diabetes every year.[1] Although there are many similarities between how both types are treated and managed, some differences do exist. Focusing on type 1 diabetes treatment and management is often done, since this is the one most often found in children and teenagers.

SYMPTOMS

Not knowing you have diabetes can be dangerous. That's why it's so important for everyone to be able to recognize the symptoms and warning signs of the disease and to make sure that anyone who has them brings them to the attention of a doctor as soon as possible.

Classic symptoms of type 1 diabetes include constant thirst and the need to urinate, extreme hunger, weight loss, fatigue, blurred vision, difficulty concentrating, skin infections, slow-healing wounds, and numbness or tingling in your feet. Sometimes these symptoms are ignored or overlooked. If that is done, the following more serious symptoms can develop: confusion, short and fast breathing, sweet or fruity smell in the breath, loss of coordination, pain in the belly, shaking, slurred speech, passing out, nausea, vomiting, and a fast heartbeat. If you have these symptoms, diabetes has advanced to

SUGAR

You don't only get glucose from table sugar, candy, and soft drinks. Sugars are also found in fruits and vegetables. Your body actually makes glucose out of any carbohydrate, particularly starches, such as bread, pasta, and rice.

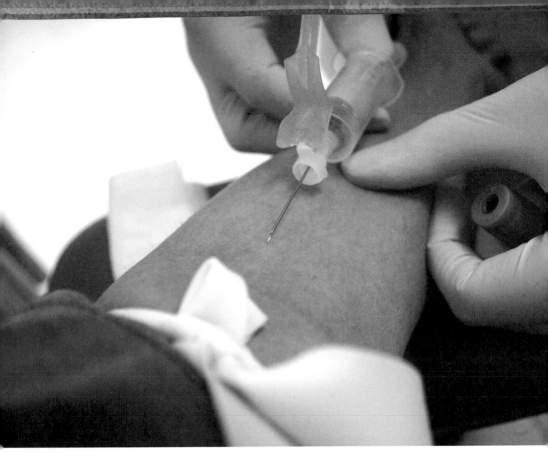

Your blood will be drawn and tested to determine if you have diabetes.

dangerous levels, and you should seek medical attention immediately.

GOING TO THE DOCTOR

If you have several of these symptoms, get to a doctor as soon as possible to be tested for diabetes. The most important thing you can bring to your doctor's appointment is information about yourself. New medicines or vitamins and changes in diet should certainly be discussed.

When a doctor suspects you have diabetes, he or she will examine many different things—urine, blood pressure, and temperature, for example. But these have more to do with your overall health (and whether you're in any immediate danger) than to determine if you have diabetes. For that, doctors must test your blood. If the results indicate that you have diabetes, you may need to be admitted to the hospital for more

BLOOD SUGAR TESTS

Tests that examine blood sugar include:

Fasting sugar. Usually done first thing in the morning after you haven't eaten anything since the night before. This allows doctors to see what your blood sugar is like when it should normally be low. This test is primarily done to screen patients for type 2 diabetes.

Random sugar. Done at any time to determine how your blood sugar level varies at different time. This test can detect diabetes if the blood sugar is very high and can be used to diagnose type 1 or type 2 diabetes.

Oral glucose tolerance test. This is usually done in the morning after you don't eat or drink anything past midnight on the previous night. Your blood sugar is then tested. Then you drink a certain amount of liquid containing glucose and your blood is tested many times afterward, at 30–60 minute intervals. This test is primarily done to diagnose patients with type 2 diabetes.

Hemoglobin A1c test. This test measures how much sugar is "stuck" to your red blood cells. It gives an estimate of how high your blood sugars have been over the life span of a red blood cell (approximately the past 120 days). Commonly used to monitor patients already diagnosed with diabetes, the test has also been used lately to diagnose diabetes.

intensive treatment to lower your blood sugars and stabilize your body's systems.

Once diabetes is diagnosed, you will have regular follow-up appointments with your doctor and probably also with a diabetes educator. After your initial diabetes symptoms disappear, you may struggle with low blood sugar and maintaining levels after you eat certain kinds of foods. At this time, it is important to keep a notebook to record these problems and keep track of your meals and exercise patterns. It is best to keep a list with you at all times, where you can jot down any changes or concerns you have as they come up. Also keep track of changes in your life and bring this up in your appointments as well. New friends, new neighborhood, new classes, and new hobbies (particularly active sports) can bring changes and your doctor should be informed.

STILL LIVE YOUR LIFE

Having diabetes will change your life. You'll have to be vigilant about monitoring your food intake and blood sugar levels, because it will be up to you to manage the things your body can no longer manage on its own. It will be time-consuming and may be frustrating at times, but it is not the end of the world by any means.

DIABETES BY THE NUMBERS

- **25.8 million: the number of children and adults in the United States who have diabetes[2]**
- **8.3 percent: the percentage of people in the United States who have diabetes[3]**
- **3 million: the number of Americans who may have type 1 diabetes[4]**
- **More than 15,000: the number of children diagnosed with type 1 diabetes in the United States every year[5]**
- **366 million: the number of people worldwide that the United Nations predicts will have diabetes by 2030[6]**

While there is not yet a cure for diabetes, many new therapeutic advances are allowing millions of kids just like you to go on with their lives, much as before. You can still live your life the way you want—hanging out with friends, being involved in extracurricular activities, and following your dreams. But you will have to take on more responsibility. And that's why you need to be aware of what is going on as soon as possible. If allowed to continue without proper management, diabetes can make you very sick, or worse. So be smart, be safe, and be healthy by getting medical attention as soon as symptoms arise.

ASK YOURSELF THIS

- *What symptoms did you have that led you to see a doctor?*

- *When you first visited the doctor, did he or she suspect diabetes before you had blood tests?*

- *When first diagnosed with diabetes, how much did you know about the disease?*

- *How long have you had diabetes? How has it impacted your life? How do you still take part in the activities you most enjoy?*

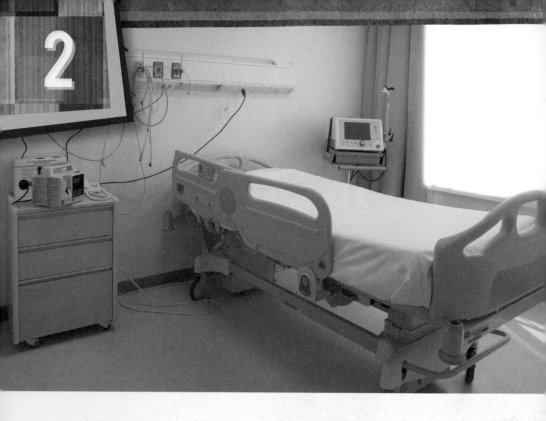

WHY ME? CAUSES AND RISK FACTORS

O livia sat up in her hospital bed, trying to concentrate on the small TV that hung over her bed from an adjustable metal arm. Even though her favorite program was on— it had always made her laugh—she could barely crack a smile. Around her were flowers and a

If your diabetes is not discovered early enough, your diagnosis may come after a trip to the hospital.

goofy get-well card signed by all her classmates. Her friends and family had been good about visiting, and since arriving at the hospital, she wasn't feeling as sick as she had been before. Still, when the evening physician briskly entered the room and said, "How are we doing tonight, Ollie?" she burst into tears.

"Why did I get diabetes, Dr. Moore?" she cried. "What did I do wrong?"

Dr. Moore put down Olivia's chart, pulled up a chair, and held Olivia's shaking hand.

"Oh, Ollie, no," she said soothingly. "You didn't do anything."

"But I feel like it's my fault, that I wasn't careful and . . . and . . ."

"Ollie, while we know a lot about why older people get diabetes, science has yet to discover what causes the type 1 diabetes that you have," Dr. Moore told her. "It might be something in your genes, some germ, or even something in the air. We don't really know. So even if you knew everything that the best scientists know, there wouldn't be that much that you could have done differently."

"But will I ever get better?" Olivia sniffled.

"Ollie, you *are* getting better," the doctor replied, waving Olivia's chart. "Remember how sick you were when you came here? Thanks to the insulin, your blood sugar is returning to normal levels. And soon, you'll be able to take care of your insulin yourself. And who knows? Maybe one day soon, you'll be able to get rid of your diabetes for good."

CAUSES

Ollie felt she did something to get her disease, but it's not her fault that she got type 1 diabetes, as Dr. Moore explained to her. So, how and why *do* you get diabetes and what can you do to prevent it?

Scientists still have a lot to learn about diabetes, but they are fairly certain that genes play some role in the development of the disease. But genes don't explain the whole story and having the gene for diabetes doesn't guarantee that you'll come down with the disease. There probably also has to be

"One of the greatest challenges for Type 1 diabetes . . . is really understanding the most fundamental aspects of what causes the disease and the biology around the pancreas and islets themselves. I see us really moving more directly in this area, really trying to get at the fundamental processes that determine why the immune system destroys beta cells in some people and not in others."[1]

—*Jeffrey A. Bluestone, PhD, UCSF Executive Vice Chancellor and Provost; AW and Mary Clausen Distinguished Professor of Medicine, Pathology, Microbiology & Immunology* a trigger, which is something that sets off the disease, much like lighting a fuse will set off a firecracker. Many scientists believe that a virus triggers type 1 diabetes—likely in people who are already susceptible to the disease because of genes or other reasons. But the frustrating thing is that so far, nobody can really say for sure what causes type 1 diabetes.

GENES

At least 18 genetic locations, known as IDDM1–IDDM18, have been discovered to have some connection to type 1 diabetes. Not surprisingly, many of these genes affect your immune response. However, having one of these "diabetes genes" only increases your risk slightly. It does not mean you will ever develop diabetes.

More is known about type 2 diabetes' causes and risk factors. Doctors know that certain factors such as being overweight can lead to developing type 2 diabetes. Knowing these risk factors allows you to take preventative action—that is, you can exercise and watch your weight to help prevent type 2 diabetes.

Not knowing what causes type 1 diabetes makes it hard to say how to prevent getting it. Of course, this doesn't mean that you shouldn't bother maintaining a good program of physical fitness and a proper diet. There are many good reasons why that's a good idea. Even if you do contract diabetes, having a healthy body means

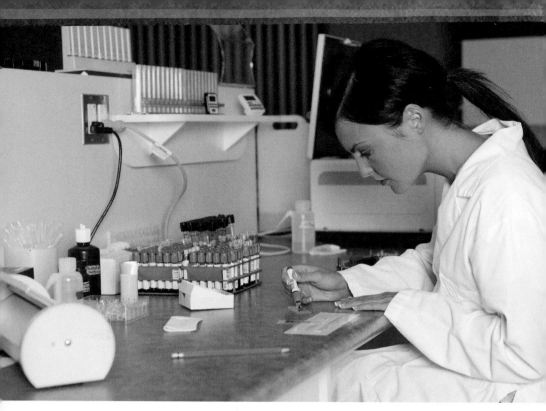
Scientists continue researching to find a cause of type 1 diabetes.

you'll be able to deal with it better. Also, even if weight doesn't put you at risk for diabetes now, it can put you at risk for type 2 when you get older. More teenagers are starting to have a condition known as prediabetes, which means they are at risk for developing type 2 diabetes when they get older.

RISK FACTORS

What are some of the risk factors for developing type 1 diabetes? Males are slightly more likely to develop it than females, and Caucasian youth are more at risk than others. If there are other diabetics in your family, your risk of getting diabetes is higher than if your parents did not have the disease. But do not totally freak out, because even with a diabetic parent, your chances of getting diabetes are less than one in ten.[2] That said, if diabetes is in your family, you should monitor yourself closely for any symptoms of the disease.

Having other autoimmune disorders, whether they are present in you or your family members, can also put you at a higher risk. Find out if you have or have ever had Graves' disease, Hashimoto's thyroiditis (a form of hypothyroidism), Addison's disease, multiple

MYTHS ABOUT THE CAUSES OF TYPE 1 DIABETES

1. Too much sugar or a bad diet.
   While controlling your sugar intake and maintaining a healthy diet is always a good idea, there is no evidence that any kind of food—including sugar—causes type 1 diabetes. Too much sugar, fat, and other unhealthy substances *can* result in obesity, which in turn can lead to type 2 diabetes or other related conditions such as prediabetes.

2. Stress.
   Too much stress is not good for you, and while it may make the symptoms worse for those who already have diabetes, there is no evidence that diabetes is directly caused by stress.

3. Catching it from other diabetics.
   Diabetes is not contagious at all, so there is no risk of catching it from another diabetic.

You are at a higher risk to get diabetes if your father has the disease than if your mother has the disease.

sclerosis (MS), or pernicious anemia. Other risk factors include being sick often as a baby, having been born when your mother was older, and having a mother who had preeclampsia, an abnormally high blood pressure condition, when she was pregnant with you.

Although these factors lead to a higher chance of getting diabetes, it's important to distinguish that they do not cause diabetes. Conversely, having none of these risk factors doesn't mean you won't get diabetes, either. Your best option is to pay attention to your body, know the symptoms and watch for them, know the risk factors that you can control, and act accordingly. But just remember, even if you have diabetes, it's okay. Science is improving all the time, and treatment makes managing your disease very achievable.

ASK YOURSELF THIS

- *Have you ever blamed yourself for developing diabetes? What did you think you could have done differently?*

- *When you have diabetes, do you think it's more helpful to dwell on the past or plan for the future? Why?*

- *How do you feel about the fact that there is no known cause for type 1 diabetes?*

- *What risk factors did you have for developing diabetes? Did you know before you were diagnosed about these risks? Why or why not?*

PREDIABETES

While type 1 diabetes can come on with little or no warning and cannot be avoided, with type 2, there may be some warning in the form of a condition called prediabetes. Here, blood sugar is high but not high enough to be considered diabetes. Some of the symptoms may be similar (frequent thirst and urination). However, with greater exercise and attention to diet, developing type 2 diabetes can be prevented.

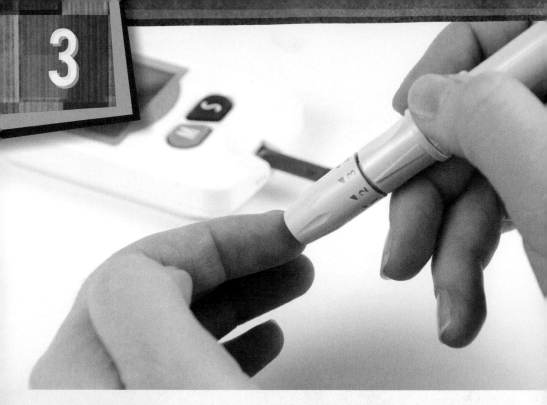

BEING RESPONSIBLE: TREATMENT AND MANAGEMENT

For the first time since he was admitted to the hospital, Terrell's head was spinning. But this time, it wasn't because of something his body was doing. Now it was spinning because the doctors and nurses started teaching him all the things he would have

To test your blood sugar levels, you have to prick your finger to get a blood sample.

to know to take care of himself once he left. Insulin, hemoglobin A1c, blood sugar levels, and the different drugs, products, and strategies—not to mention all the things he had to learn about food. It was like taking a really hard biology class—only this wasn't about getting a high grade. Here, if he got something wrong, he could make himself very sick.

"When you have diabetes type 1, the two important things your body no longer does—monitor blood sugar and produce insulin accordingly—are going to be your responsibility," his doctor explained. "Lucky for you, we live in an age where we have the tools to help replace those functions."

The staff showed Terrell how to prick his finger with a lancet, catch a drop of blood on a strip, and put it into a meter that told him his blood sugar level. They explained what the numbers meant. Terrell also learned how to give himself injections of insulin.

As he learned to monitor his blood sugar and carefully inject himself, Terrell switched to a more flexible treatment method that let him eat whenever he liked. A year later, he got an electronic pump to wear under his shirt, which pumped precise amounts of insulin directly under his skin. He still had to prick his finger many times a day to test his sugar level, though. He looked forward to one day getting a continuous glucose monitor that checked his blood all day long. *In the meantime, it wasn't too bad*, he thought, as he bit into a piece of pizza.

NEW RESPONSIBILITY

As Terrell experienced, it's a little overwhelming to suddenly have such a big responsibility thrust upon you—the responsibility of maintaining the functions that your pancreas can't, so you can stay alive and healthy. It's as if you have a new body and have to learn how to take care of it all over again. That's a handful, even in the best of times. The good news is that you'll learn how to sense what's happening in your body so you know how to react.

"Both children and adults like me who live with type 1 diabetes need to be mathematicians, physicians, personal trainers and dieticians all rolled into one. We need to be constantly factoring and adjusting, making frequent finger sticks to check blood sugars, and giving ourselves multiple daily insulin injections just to stay alive."[1]

—Mary Tyler Moore, International Chairman, Juvenile Diabetes Research Foundation

BLOOD SUGAR MONITORING

One main component of managing your diabetes involves

monitoring your blood sugar level. Your blood sugar level is the exact amount of glucose dissolved in your blood. Your goal for treatment will always be to keep your blood sugar level as steady as possible, without spikes that are too high or low.

Blood sugar levels are frequently tested each day. To find out current glucose levels, you'll likely use a glucometer. This is a device that can measure your blood sugar from a small drop of blood. You'll prick your fingertip and place the blood onto a test strip that is inserted into the glucometer. This whole process only takes a minute or two. At the beginning, you may feel more comfortable doing this in private (in a bathroom or a private room), but eventually

HISTORY OF DIABETES TREATMENT

Less than 100 years ago, if you were a diabetic, there really wasn't much anyone could do about it. As a matter of fact, until around 1900, people didn't understand what had actually gone wrong with them. After that, scientists started quickly putting the pieces together. In 1922, insulin was successfully used to treat the first patients with diabetes. From there, advancements in needles, different and better kinds of insulin, and a better understanding of the disease provided for better treatment options. The first blood sugar meters were invented in the 1960s and were commonly used by the 1980s. There has been rapid advancement in the ability to control diabetes with new insulins, insulin pumps, and better glucose monitoring over the last ten to 15 years.

*Place a bit of your blood on the glucometer
strip to determine your blood sugar levels.*

it will become so second nature that you will test
wherever you are.

A continuous glucose monitor is a newer
technology that you may also begin using
someday. For this, a sensor with an electrode
is placed just under the skin (usually on the
stomach). You will place the sensor yourself
using an injector device, which feels similar to
giving yourself an insulin injection. The sensor
is changed every three to four days. This
system still requires daily finger prick glucose
measurements for calibration and to confirm
when blood sugar readings are very high or

very low. The sensor under the skin sends the reading to a separate monitor that is about the size of a pager. This monitor can alarm the user when blood sugars are rising or falling, so you can prevent them from getting really high or low. For effective management of type 1 diabetes, you will need to check blood sugars at least four, and sometimes up to six to ten, times per day.

Doctors will also want to determine your blood sugar level control over long periods. To find this information, they'll use a hemoglobin A1c, a type of blood test. A number below 6.5 percent is considered ideal and indicates that your blood sugars are generally well controlled; 5.5 percent is normal for nondiabetics.

GETTING INSULIN

With type 1 diabetes, you need to take insulin every day. Insulin is needed for baseline control of blood sugars, to prevent high blood sugars after a meal, and to help lower blood sugars if they become elevated. Unfortunately, you cannot take insulin as a pill because the digestive process in the stomach and intestines would destroy the insulin. The only way to get insulin into your body is through an injection. The insulin is given just under the skin and is absorbed from there into the bloodstream, where it can travel throughout the body. There are two ways to get this insulin under the skin: injections using syringes or insulin pens and insulin pumps.

Syringes or insulin pens are used to inject insulin under the skin. Using a syringe, you draw up insulin from a bottle and then inject the insulin just under the skin of your stomach, legs, or arms with a small, attached needle. An insulin pen looks like a normal pen and uses a cartridge of insulin. You dial in the amount of insulin you want to inject, push a button on the pen to activate the needle, and deliver the injection. You'll need to administer several injections each day, usually on a regular schedule.

THE STORY OF INSULIN

For much of the twentieth century, diabetics had cows and pigs to thank for their survival. Once insulin was discovered to be the mechanism by which the body processes sugar and that diabetics were deficient in this important hormone, scientists concluded that by reintroducing insulin back into the body, it could help the body process sugar and counteract the effects of diabetes. A group of Canadian scientists made that discovery in 1921: Fredrick G. Banting, Charles H. Best, J. J. R. Macleod, and James B. Collip. One year later, the first human was treated with insulin—derived from the pancreas of a cow! These scientists refused to profit from their important lifesaving discovery. So, any company wanting to produce it could do so. Insulin was largely purified from pig pancreas until 1980, when a new process was found to create synthetic human insulin. Many further refinements of insulin have been made over the recent decades, giving us the many types of insulin available today.

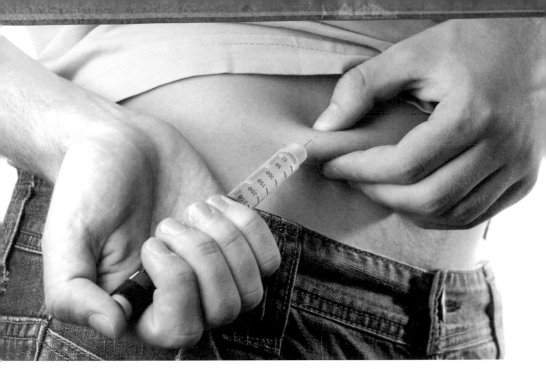

Insulin is often injected into the skin of the stomach.

The other way to get insulin into your body is through an insulin pump. A pump is an electronic device smaller than a cell phone. Attached to the pump is a plastic tube called a cannula, which is inserted into the body usually around the stomach, thighs, or buttocks, and then taped in place. The device is then clipped to your pant waist or tucked in your pocket.

The insulin pump delivers insulin to the body at a continuous rate. You can then deliver additional insulin when you eat or have a high blood sugar level that needs to be treated. You will enter information about what you eat and what your blood sugar readings are and the pump helps calculate how much additional insulin you need. You'll okay the pump to deliver a one-time shot of that additional insulin through the same cannula. Insulin pumps provide greater flexibility than injections, though the cannula does have to be changed every couple days.

MORE ABOUT INSULIN

There are different types of insulin: basal and bolus. You will take basal insulin, which is long lasting and meant as a foundation to cover your daily insulin needs. You will also take a bolus, which is fast acting and used to match the carbohydrates or glucose in the food you eat or to help lower your blood sugar when it is too high.

SENSING LOW BLOOD SUGAR

While insulin is important to lower blood sugar levels when they're high, sometimes you can "overshoot" and the insulin will lower blood sugars too much. Low blood sugars can also occur when you aren't eating on your normal schedule, during exercise, or in times of stress. This is called hypoglycemia. An important step in managing your diabetes is starting to tune in to your body so you can sense when you have hypoglycemia. Early symptoms include hunger, shakiness, nervousness, sweating, dizziness, light-headedness, and sleepiness. Check in with

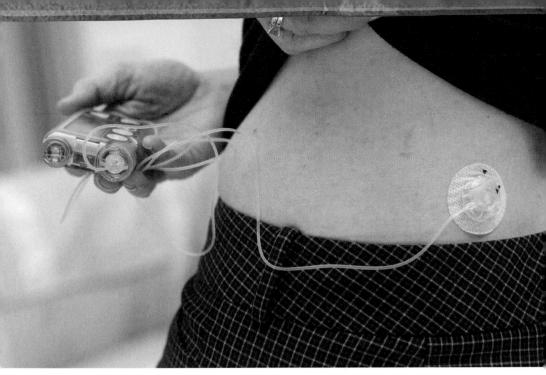

An insulin pump provides a slow, constant release of insulin rather than a single injection that lasts for many hours.

your body often, and if you feel any of these symptoms, check your glucometer to confirm your blood sugar is low and treat it immediately. Your goal is to catch low blood sugar before symptoms become more severe, leading to confusion, poor coordination, slurred speech, and passing out.

It is important that friends and family members recognize the symptoms of falling blood sugar. Teach them what you know and ask that they watch out for those symptoms in you. The more lows you have, the harder it gets to sense them. Then you can get in real trouble, because the early warning signs, such as sweating and shaking, do not occur. This condition is called hypoglycemia unawareness. If you start to become hypoglycemic unaware, you'll need to test your blood sugar levels even more frequently.

TYPES OF INSULIN

There are dozens of brands and types of insulin, and your health-care team will help you decide which is right for you. Generally, though, insulin falls into the following categories:

Rapid-acting:
- Quick onset and short duration
- Taken to cover meals in conjunction with longer-acting shot
- Taken right at the time of meals

Short-acting:
- Slightly longer onset
- Taken to cover meals eaten with 1/2–1 hour

Intermediate-acting:
- Slow onset (1–2 hours) with long duration
- Intended for daytime or overnight coverage
- Often taken with a faster/shorter-acting insulin

Long-acting:
- Slow onset and long duration
- Intended for all-day baseline coverage
- Can also be used with short/rapid acting insulin to cover meals.

Pre-mixed:
- Combination of short- and intermediate-acting insulin in measured doses
- Usually taken with meals

GETTING THE HANG OF IT

The treatment may seem like a lot, and sometimes it can be. You'll probably experience frustrating times when you're overwhelmed with checking your blood sugar or confused about if you need to eat more or less sugar. Try not to get discouraged, because soon you will figure things out and treatment will go smoothly. With each scientific and technological advancement, diabetes treatment becomes better and easier. And yes, if you keep your eye on the research horizon, you'll see that there are many promising research areas that may someday result in a permanent cure.

ASK YOURSELF THIS

- *How did you feel when you first learned everything you had to do to manage your diabetes? How did you cope with those feelings?*

- *What kind of diabetes treatment are you on? How are they working for you?*

- *Does the lack of a cure for diabetes type 1 ever discourage you? How do you keep a positive attitude about your situation?*

- *Do you think there's anything people could do to help find a cure faster? What would that be?*

IT'S ALL ABOUT THE FOOD: DIET AND NUTRITION

To nearly everyone at the picnic, the table was a buffet of delightful treats—hot dogs, hamburgers, cookies, potato chips, cake, and soft drinks. But to Bandhu, it was mostly carbs. It wasn't like he was absolutely forbidden to eat anything there, but the realities

No foods are off limits, but you'll need to watch your blood sugar more carefully with some foods.

of living with type 1 diabetes made him look at carbs as "the enemy." After all, eating anything on that table could quickly dump a whole bunch of sugar into his blood, causing his levels to spike. That meant he would need to test his blood, inject insulin to lower his blood sugar level accordingly, then test again, to make sure he still wasn't too high or had gone too low.

In the year since he'd been diagnosed, however, Bandhu really got the hang of counting carbs. He had also become an expert at reading food labels, not just for the carbohydrate content, but also for protein, fat, fiber, and other elements that can affect the sugar in his blood. At home, things were less of a problem, of course. His parents helped him figure out what he could and could not eat, and he could always read labels.

Parties such as this one, where food wasn't always labeled, were a bit trickier. For times like these, and for restaurants as well, he kept a little pocket nutrition guide. On this day, Bandhu had prepared himself for the party by decreasing his carb intake that day. He gave himself a bolus shot of insulin and carefully measured out precise spoonfuls of ice cream using a measuring spoon from the kitchen. He was glad to see there were at least plenty of sugar-free

Being able to identify carbs and measure portions accurately will simplify the process of determining how much insulin will cover your meal.

sodas and even better, a bowl of peanuts, which contained a low amount of carbs. He knew he could eat those a little more freely. As he popped a handful of peanuts in his mouth, he thought, *I guess this isn't that bad.*

NEW EATING PLAN

Lots of people think being diabetic means you can never eat sugar, but that is not true. With the introduction of fast-acting insulin (and particularly the insulin pump), there is hardly anything you absolutely can't eat in small portions, provided you balance it with whatever else you eat that day and adjust your insulin intake accordingly.

Still, you do have to pay more attention to your diet and understand what is in the foods you eat. This is particularly true of sugars and carbohydrates, which the body quickly converts into sugar and sends into your bloodstream. Being consistent with your diet will decrease the chance of unexpected surprises.

You will have to start counting carbs, so you don't eat too many or too few. Not all carbs are the same, however. Simple carbohydrates, such as those in candy bars and soft drinks, cause blood sugar to rise very quickly. Complex carbohydrates, such as those found in wheat bread and rice, cause blood sugar to rise more slowly. You'll want to eat more complex carbs and fewer simple carbs whenever possible.

To get an accurate count of carbohydrate content, study the nutritional

NOT ALL CARBS ARE CREATED EQUAL—THE GLYCEMIC INDEX

The latest advance in helping diabetics plan their meals is the glycemic index. This rather complicated calculation tells you how greatly and how rapidly a given food will cause your blood sugar to rise. High numbers refer to faster carbs; low numbers work slower. Some health conscious food companies list it on their food labels.

labels on food packaging. Of course, when you go to other people's homes or restaurants, where there aren't any packages to read, it's a different story. Not every place is sensitive to what diabetics have to deal with (although, thankfully, more and more are getting a clue), so you might want to buy a nutritional guide at your bookstore or library and carry it with you. Then you'll always have something handy to consult. Cell phone apps can also aid in carb counting.

Your doctor will probably encourage you to spread out your eating as much as possible over the day. This will keep your glucose levels relatively steady. You will also need to have an emergency sugar supply—glucose tablets, sugar packets, juice—at all times, to consume if your blood sugar is low. Before going to bed, you'll need to check your blood sugar and maybe have a snack if it is low to avoid lows in the middle of the night.

VEGETARIAN DIABETIC

What about vegetarians and vegans? Do they have special concerns? Actually, in terms of controlling your blood sugar level, a vegetarian or vegan diet is usually significantly higher in fiber. For a diabetic, the more fiber in a food, the better, as it will directly offset the increase in blood sugar from carbs. That is, you can subtract the grams of fiber from the grams of carbs during your carbohydrate count. However, vegetarians need to be careful to avoid too many carbs, since most of their food often comes from carbohydrate sources rather than meat or protein sources.

You will also need to be aware of how proteins can have a delayed effect on raising your blood sugar, while fat can slow down the rate at which carbohydrates raise blood sugar. For example, restaurant Chinese food served with rice and noodles is loaded with carbohydrates. But it can also be high in fat. The high fat content leads to a delay in the spike of the blood sugar.

> "Having accurate carb counts helps tremendously. If I have to eat out, I try to pick places that I have had good luck with in regards to carb counting. It is amazing how many places don't offer nutritional information. Sometimes you really do have to just take a guess based off of other foods that are similar. It isn't perfect, and I have certainly calculated meals wrong. Diabetes isn't a perfect science. Especially in a world that seems so adamant on making it difficult."[1]
>
> *—Danielle, 20, diagnosed with type 1 diabetes at age 17*

In sum, for diabetics, while sugar is not strictly forbidden, eating too much of it is not a good idea—but that's how it is for anyone. Sugary snacks such as soda and candy are not healthful food choices and provide no positive nutritional benefits. Many types of fiber help control a rise in your blood sugar (and also help fight against cholesterol), so eating lots of fiber-rich foods (whole grains, beans, and many kinds of fruits and vegetables) is highly recommended. But

A proper diet for type 1 diabetes is the same as it is for everyone—a balanced variety of healthful foods.

guess what? Everyone needs lots of fiber. If weight gain is a problem, you will also have to be extra careful about empty calories and fatty foods. Also, because diabetics are more prone to heart and other cardiovascular problems, you're going to be in charge of keeping an eye on your cholesterol too. Keeping your weight up, if that's a problem, will require tweaking your diet. Careful monitoring and the advice of a doctor or nutritionist will help you get it right. Once you have your own nutritional system down, you can allow yourself to indulge in some treats on special occasions by adjusting your diet and your insulin. Bon appétit!

ASK YOURSELF THIS

- *How important is what you eat to your overall happiness?*

- *What are your favorite foods? How do you integrate them into your diabetic diet?*

- *In what ways has diabetes changed the way you look at food? Do you eat more or less than you did before you were diagnosed?*

- *Would you like to see changes in the way food is packaged and served? What are they?*

SUGAR-FREE GUM

You might have noticed sorbitol, isomalt, or xylitol on the ingredient list on some sugar-free products, particularly chewing gum. These artificial sweeteners are among the substances known as sugar alcohols. Besides having fewer calories than real sugar, they don't need insulin to be metabolized. This makes them a great choice for diabetics!

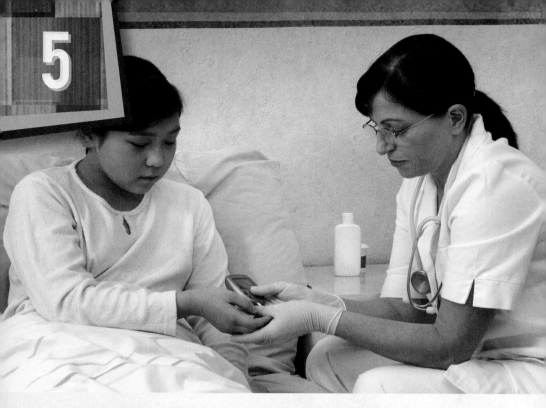

5

LIVING ON THE EDGE: POTENTIAL COMPLICATIONS

J un didn't remember anything about how she came to be sitting on the floor in the school's hallway. She recalled leaving chemistry class, but her classmates filled her in on the other details, like how she started talking funny and suddenly burst into tears. Then she

Ignoring signs of low blood sugar can lead you to the school nurse's office, as Jun found, or even to the hospital.

slumped to the ground, conscious, but unable to stand. The school nurse saw what happened and knowing that Jun was diabetic, got her a sports drink containing glucose.

"What happened?" she asked. But she thought she already knew the answer.

"Looks like a blood sugar low snuck up on you, Jun," the nurse responded. It's what every diabetic has to watch out for, though everything lately seemed to have been fine. After a few weeks of trial and error, Jun thought she had managed to find the perfect combination of medications and dosages. What went wrong?

"Sometimes you can catch some early hints, like maybe you're sweating too much or feeling dizzy or starting to shake, but you might have missed all that," the nurse explained. "Perhaps you might want to make an appointment with your regular physician."

Later that week, Jun was at her doctor's office repeating what had happened in school. He decided to run a few extra tests, but, luckily, they all checked out okay.

"Everything seems all right, Jun," her doctor told her. "We're going to make a few adjustments to your dosage and I'm going to recommend that you check your glucose more frequently."

Jun left the office relieved, vowing to be more vigilant about checking her levels.

WHAT CAN HAPPEN IF YOU'RE NOT DILIGENT WITH TREATMENT

Jun's story is one that almost all diabetics share. Things go well for a while and then all of a sudden, strange things start happening. Sometimes it can be really difficult to deal with. While this shouldn't discourage you from pursuing your goals and dreams and living the way you want to live, you also need to be aware of when to keep an extra watch on how you're doing.

Ironically, once you're diagnosed as a diabetic and learn how to treat yourself, your biggest challenge might not be keeping your blood sugar down—the thing that brought you

YOUR DIABETES EDUCATOR

While you will rely on your physician to treat any complications and monitor your overall progress, staying healthy and avoiding complications involves quite a bit of homework. And the teacher who will help you understand your disease and how to manage it is your diabetes educator. He or she is usually a registered nurse who is specially trained to help you take care of yourself and answer most of the questions you might have. Diabetes educators are also in contact with your doctors. That way, everyone on your medical team knows the necessary facts about your health and they can work together to create a management program that works best for you.

Stress can lower or raise your blood sugar levels, so be sure to monitor closely during times of high stress.

to the doctor in the first place—but keeping it up. Things such as stress, physical activity, and some medications can unexpectedly lower blood sugar. Even the most precise insulin pump sometimes lowers blood sugar too far or too rapidly, often through human dosage error or not taking into account all relevant factors. This is sometimes known as an insulin reaction.

While a healthy pancreas can produce a hormone called glucagon to raise blood sugar when it falls too low, this process does not operate normally in diabetics. Glucagon acts in direct opposition to the action of insulin and helps the body release stored sugars from the liver and muscles. The treatment for low blood sugar is to immediately consume a small amount of something containing glucose, if not glucose tablets itself. For emergency cases, a friend, family member, or medical professional can directly inject synthetic glucagon into your bloodstream. After that, a physician might recommend modifications to your medications, dosage, blood testing schedule, diet, exercise plan, or other aspect of your treatment. It's not just about trial and error, although that might be a larger part of your treatment in the early stages. You also have to recognize that your treatment is a dynamic process. Your body, after all, is growing and developing, your lifestyle and schedule change, and even your mental state might be different. All of those factors can affect your blood sugar levels and because

"There are all the common horror stories related to diabetic complications, but there are other, smaller things that no one who doesn't have diabetes would think about. Other kids were getting over being afraid of the boogeyman and learning to brave the dark, and I was terrified I wouldn't wake up in the morning. It's a very alarming feeling, waking up [with low blood sugar]. It's very strange, everything is disconnected. At times when I'm low at night, especially if I'm in bed, my legs will feel strange, like they want to move, and then they twitch on their own. I've tried to keep my legs still, because it really freaks me out, but there doesn't seem to be anything I can do to stop it."[1]

—*Anna, 17, diagnosed with type 1 diabetes at age 10*

your body cannot adjust its responses automatically, you have to make those adjustments instead.

LONG-TERM COMPLICATIONS

You probably noticed that once Jun was in the doctor's office, her doctor ordered other tests that did not test her blood sugar. That's because, while low blood sugar might be an ever-present concern, there are other long-term effects of diabetes, many of which progress very slowly and require constant vigilance. They involve every area and system of your body. Because these all involve different medical specialties, your diabetes health-care team may involve a few different kinds of doctors.

DIABULIMIA

Taking insulin is serious business and no deviations from the prescribed times and doses should occur without consulting your physician. A disturbing trend that goes against this advice is a condition known as diabulimia, which may affect as many as three out of ten diabetics.[2] Diabulimia is a condition whereby diabetics, often teenage girls, intentionally take a lower dose of insulin so their blood sugar remains high, causing abnormal weight loss. Like any eating disorder, diabulimia can be life threatening. If you have any diabulimic tendencies or know anyone who does, get help immediately.

EYES, NERVES, AND KIDNEY DAMAGE

Eyes need to be checked for diabetic retinopathy, which is the overgrowth of the blood vessels or bleeding into the retina at the back of the eye. They should also be checked for signs of glaucoma or cataracts.

Erratic blood sugar can affect nerves, so they must be tested frequently, particularly for loss of sensation in the feet. Doctors will ask about a "falling asleep" sensation in the feet, which could be a sign of diabetic neuropathy, and may test your ability to feel different sensations in your feet. Ingrown toenails, for instance, can be a problem because they can lead to pain and infections that aren't noticed when the nerves are damaged. Loss of sensation and circulation can lead to calluses, ulcers, and other problems. The skin in general is more susceptible to infection. Overall, nerve damage and poor circulation to the feet can lead to infections of the skin or bone that may ultimately require removal of a toe or even an entire foot.

Kidney disease is also a complication. Doctors will test for small amounts of protein in your urine that can be an early sign of kidney damage. Poor control of blood sugar—specifically, when it is too high—is the biggest risk factor for these complications. You can

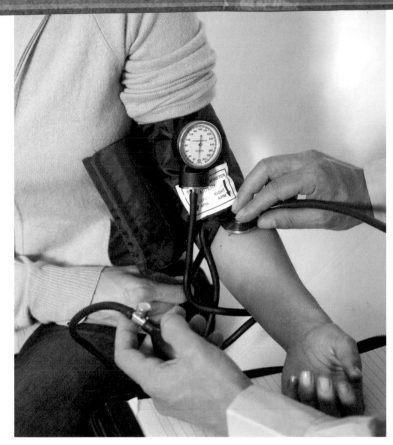

Diabetics must watch their blood pressure more carefully than other people.

significantly reduce your risk of developing them by keeping your blood sugar level under control.

BLOOD PRESSURE

Because diabetics are more vulnerable to many cardiovascular ailments—those that pertain to the heart or circulatory system—you'll need to have your blood pressure and cholesterol checked regularly, particularly to monitor high LDL, which is the bad type of cholesterol. Should blood pressure, cholesterol, or triglycerides measure too high, you will need to take action. Exercise and maintaining a healthy body weight are important ways to lower these complications without medications. Your doctor will let you know if further treatment is needed.

DIABETIC KETOACIDOSIS

Another condition diabetics must be on the lookout for is diabetic ketoacidosis (DKA). When insulin is low and the body isn't able to run on glucose, it starts breaking down fat cells for energy. This produces an acidic substance called ketones, which your body will use as fuel instead of glucose. However, too much of this acid in your bloodstream can make you very sick. Ketones can build up in your blood and also show up in your urine. If your ketones are too high, it can cause you to pass out or worse. This condition occurs when blood sugar levels have been abnormally high and

DON'T FORGET TO FLOSS

When dealing with all the medical issues associated with diabetes, it's easy to forget your teeth. Because diabetes can affect the way your body fights bacteria, it's easier to develop plaque and other dental problems. Diligent brushing and flossing is essential as well as regular trips to the dentist. Knowing your teeth and gums are healthy is a sure way to put a smile on your face.

there isn't enough insulin available. So, when blood sugars are very high for several hours, it may be advisable to test your urine with a home test kit. Most important, you can never skip your insulin or take a day off from your diabetes treatment. Even if you aren't eating, you must supply your body with insulin to prevent ketoacidosis, as skipping insulin is the most common cause of DKA. If you experience dry mouth, nausea, confusion, fruity breath, or a strange odor in your urine, get attention immediately. Although DKA is scary, most people are able to avoid this complication with careful glucose monitoring.

ASK YOURSELF THIS

- *Are you often afraid of things going wrong with your diabetes treatment? What do you do about it?*

- *What parts of your body or overall health do you feel are most affected by diabetes? How do you manage it?*

- *How much have unexpected "lows" interfered with your life? What do you do about it?*

- *Do you think it's possible to live completely without complications? Why or why not?*

6

ADJUSTMENTS HERE AND THERE: A NEW LIFESTYLE

Tonya changed into her practice clothes and tested herself one last time. A bit high, but that was okay. From experience, Tonya knew that the next 45 minutes of intense workout would more than lower that. Tonya grabbed her gym bag and rechecked it. Besides

When you play sports or exercise, have your diabetes kit handy in case of an emergency.

her towel and a bottle of water, she had her bag-within-the-bag. In it was her diabetes kit: glucometer, extra strips, emergency snacks, and an emergency glucagon injection kit. Then she went to meet up with the volleyball team.

"Okay, I think we're ready to play," Coach Willis told the team.

A couple weeks before, Tonya became dizzy and disoriented on the court because she hadn't been paying attention to how much all that exercise had lowered her blood sugar. She had always been determined not to let diabetes interfere with enjoying the things she loved, and volleyball was at the top of the list. She worried that when she brought the

WHAT'S IN YOUR BAG?

Here's a short list of the minimum supplies that every diabetic should have at all times:

- Insulin
- Syringes
- Blood glucose testing supplies
- Pump or continuous glucose monitor supplies (if you use these)
- Ketone testing strips
- Glucagon
- Glucose tablets or fast-acting sugar
- Batteries (if you use electric devices)
- Snacks
- First aid kit
- Emergency phone numbers

episode up with her doctor, he might tell her to give up sports.

"Actually, Tonya, having regular exercise like that is a good idea," he told her to her relief. "Let's just have a quick checkup to make sure there's nothing we need to be concerned about."

He also told her how keeping in shape made her heart stronger, her muscles toned, and kept her weight at a healthy range. It could also lower her chances of contracting many of the complications diabetics are prone to getting. And best of all, it was good for relieving stress. While that would be good for almost anyone, for diabetics, stress reduction is critical in maintaining proper blood sugar control and for preventing other complications.

After determining she was healthy enough to engage in strenuous exercise, he gave her some pointers about adjusting her basal

"I'm a 14-year-old athletic kid, with lots of energy! I like playing all kind of sports. Track, soccer, football, basketball. But playing them now with type 1 diabetes is a little bit different. With football, since we do more running and other stuff for practices, I usually have to check my blood sugar every 30 or so minutes during practice, because of conditioning workouts. During games, I would check it as much as I could. I would drink some apple juice, a total of about 30 carbs, so that my blood sugar would stay up during a play. Whenever I would come out for a little break, I would check my blood sugar and drink a little quick acting sugar, to keep it up."[1]

—*Joel, 14, diagnosed with type 1 diabetes at age 12*

Before starting an exercise regimen or a sport, meet with your doctor to make sure you know how diabetes and exercise will affect you.

rate and monitoring her glucose levels. Tonya needed to keep as much of an eye on those as she did on the ball. Since then, Tonya found that she seldom needed a break before halftime.

Exercise lets glucose be absorbed into the cells without the help of insulin.

EXERCISE

While there is no avoiding some of the hassles, medical and otherwise, that diabetes will probably bring, most of the time, you'll be pretty much concerned with the ho-hum task of maintenance. This refers to the day-to-day life of being a diabetic.

As most everyone knows, exercise has great benefits. Your heart, muscles, lungs, circulation, weight, and even your mood all improve when you follow some kind of exercise program. In the case of type 1 diabetes, there's an added aspect that's very important. Because exercise uses up glucose, it can be very useful in moderating your blood sugar levels, particularly after you eat; indeed, exercise is extremely close to acting how insulin acts. Because of this, you have to be careful to

BENEFITS OF BEING ACTIVE

There are many benefits to exercising and staying active throughout the day. Exercise helps your bones, muscles, and heart get stronger, and it also lowers your blood pressure. Exercise reduces stress and boosts your mood, and you'll also have more energy during the day and sleep better at night. It will keep your body at a good weight level for you too, which prevents other health problems.

monitor your glucose level and probably lower your insulin dose accordingly during times of exercise.

While you should first check with your doctor before taking on a new exercise regimen, generally speaking, unless you have other complications, any type of exercise should be okay. Consistency is the key. Which type of exercise should you do? The type you enjoy and can stick with, of course!

Keep aware, particularly when doing sports where it's sometimes difficult to take a time out, that there is the possibility of getting low blood

DIABETES AND AIRPORT SECURITY

The US Transportation Security Administration requires you to notify an officer at airport security that you have diabetes and are carrying your supplies with you. Almost all diabetes-related supplies are allowed through security checkpoints once they have been screened. If you don't want to take your pump through the metal detector, you can request a pat down inspection instead.

sugar. Frequent testing is important and having some carbs always on hand is essential. You might also find that lowering your basal rate will compensate for strenuous physical activity, particularly when you are using a pump. If you have a pump, attach it securely with tape or an elastic band when doing anything physically active.

By paying attention to your body and working with your doctor, therapist, or other health-care provider, you'll eventually figure out a system that's right for you.

STRESS MANAGEMENT

As a diabetic, it will be extra important to pay attention to how and when you become stressed. Stress can come on suddenly. A pop quiz or an argument with your parents, for example, can be instant triggers to change your blood sugar level. But, the tricky part about stress is that sometimes it can lower

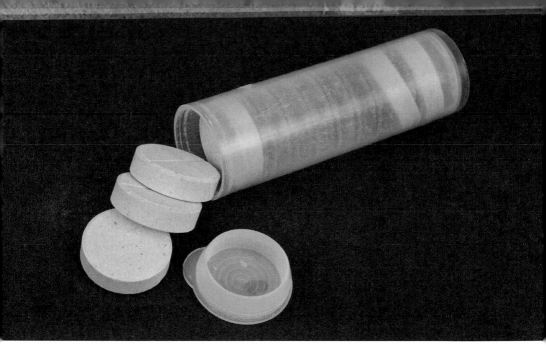

Glucose tablets serve as a quick way to raise your blood sugar.

your blood sugar and sometimes it can raise it. So when stress hits, you need to remember to check your levels so you can provide the appropriate treatment. Chronic stress—the kind that you have over a long period of time—is even unhealthier, particularly since it affects the organs and systems where diabetics are most vulnerable, leading to high blood pressure and cardiovascular disease.

Exercise, of course, is a great stress reducer and another reason why it is so important. Yoga, meditation, going for walks, playing chess, listening to calming music, or reading a book can bring your stress level down. Try a few things out to see what works best for you.

ALWAYS BE PREPARED

Vacations and other time away from home also present a few challenges. These events can be best met by observing the motto "Always be prepared." Extra supplies of insulin, testing strips, and batteries (if you use an electronic pump or meter) are a must, especially if you're going somewhere where there is the slightest chance these won't be available. As always, you should have access to some snacks. Bring a copy of your prescription, and it's also a good idea to get a letter from your doctor outlining your diagnosis and treatment. This is especially important if you are going to travel through an airport or to another country.

Bring watertight plastic bags to the pool, lake, or beach to protect your diabetes supplies against water and sand. If you go to theme parks or another kind of entertainment facility, make sure you are wearing your medical alert

WEAR YOUR MEDICAL ALERT BRACELET

It is essential that diabetics have something on them at all times that identifies them as diabetics. In case of emergency, paramedics, doctors, or bystanders can find out what is going on and take the proper action more quickly. Most people wear bracelets clearly stating that they are diabetic and any other pertinent medical information. A medical alert bracelet should also refer people to some place such as a wallet where additional information, such as contact information for your health-care team or your insulin, is kept.

necklace, bracelet, or have your wallet card with you. It probably won't take too much extra time or hassle, and it's worth the extra insurance, to know that you can be safe in case of an emergency.

ASK YOURSELF THIS

- *What's your favorite form of exercise? How often do you do it? How does that contribute to your diabetes management?*

- *Is there anything in particular that stresses you out? What is it? What do you do to calm down?*

- *Do you have a special bag where you keep all your diabetes supplies? What does it look like? Why did you choose it?*

- *Were you ever away from home when you suddenly realized you were missing something important for your diabetes treatment? What happened? What did you do?*

- *How important do you think lifestyle is in maintaining your overall health, especially since you have diabetes?*

7

FRIENDS, SCHOOL, AND INSULIN: DEALING WITH SOCIAL ISSUES

*U**ghhh, some people!* Asif thought irritably. That older kid had really ruined his meal, asking dumb questions and making ignorant comments. He had just started feeling comfortable around other people and then something like this had to happen and make him feel all weird again.

"Why do you have to wear that thing?" the kid asked Asif, after he noticed him adjusting the dial on his insulin pump. Asif informed him that he had diabetes and this was part of his treatment.

"I wouldn't wear that if I had it," he said mockingly.

"Well, then you would have to use needles to inject yourself," Asif told him.

"I wouldn't do that either," the kid said.

"Well, then you'd die," Asif told him, quickly finishing his meal and leaving the lunchroom.

Once in the hallway, Asif was mad at himself for letting himself get riled up because of someone else's ignorance about his disease. He tried to calm himself, since he knew that getting angry and frustrated didn't do his blood sugar level any good.

"Hey, Asif," Evan greeted him. "Want to hit the court after school for some one-on-one?" Although Asif wasn't feeling all that sociable, he figured that shooting hoops might take his mind off that jerk at lunch.

"Sure, I'll meet you at the court," Asif said. As he walked to next period, Asif found himself starting to calm down about the lunchroom. His real friends didn't care at all about his diabetes, anyway.

TELLING OTHERS

Diabetes is nothing to be ashamed of, yet, one of the hardest things you may encounter after being diagnosed is telling other people you have it. You might feel a sense of embarrassment about having a disease and all that it entails. Some people might think you did something to catch it or assume you're out of shape and developed the disease because of that. But of course, these aren't true. Sometimes people might stare as you prick your finger, fiddle with your pump, or inject yourself with a needle or insulin pen. Some diabetics are so nervous to tell others, they even keep their diabetes a secret from their best friends or people they're dating.

"I think one of the hardest parts with friends is when you go to parties. You're likely to have twenty or so people all staring at you while you take your insulin, sometimes even laughing or teasing you about it. Most of the time I just don't eat anything and avoid the teasing, but it can get really annoying. Luckily, every once in awhile you get one of those great people who will stand up for you and tell people off for it, or will help distract them so that they won't see. I love it when I get friends like that."[1]

—*Kaylene, 17, diagnosed with type 1 diabetes at age 11*

While you might want to say that your medical condition is nobody's business but your own, there are very important reasons why it's necessary to let others know about your diabetes and even educate them about your treatment, particularly the people you see all the time. The most important of these reasons is that,

THE LIMITS OF SHARING

Each diabetic decides how many details to share about the experience of having the disease. Much of that is up to you, but what you should never waver on is sharing needles, medication, or other equipment that is prescribed for you. This is dangerous to both you and the other party and, in many places, illegal. Regardless of the pressure you may feel from someone to do so or how badly you might want to be accepted by some group, do not do it.

should you suddenly dip into a low, you need to make sure that others around you are aware of what to do to bring you back to normal. Not doing so might save you from embarrassment, but doing so might save your life!

The most important people to tell after your family (who obviously are usually the first to know), are teachers and students at school, and anyone you work with if you have a job. They will need to understand your special needs in terms of medication, supplies, and diet, and it's also a good idea to educate them about what to do in case of a hypoglycemic emergency. You

Talk to your friends about your diabetes. It's important they know about your condition and what to do in case of an emergency.

might even consider having a nurse or some other health-care professional come to your school and give a presentation. Many diabetes organizations provide materials to schools and other organizations explaining the important information to help students who are diabetic.

THEY'RE JUST TRYING TO HELP

You might also encounter problems with people who know you have diabetes but don't understand various aspects of how the disease is managed. Like many diabetics, you've probably had the experience of reaching for a cookie or something sweet and somebody tells you, "Hey, you're not allowed to eat that!" Of course, you know you can. In these situations, it's best to be calm and patient—that person is only trying to help you—and explain to him or her why it's okay. Remember, before you developed diabetes, you probably didn't understand much about this disease either, so before you react negatively, take the time to understand where people are coming from.

DEALING WITH PARENTS

As children become teenagers, they often get into conflicts with their parents as they try to assert their independence. Teens don't want their moms or dads to control every little thing anymore. With diabetics, this conflict can involve managing the disease—with teens believing they can handle it themselves and parents having anxiety about leaving such serious matters to their children. Certainly, as children grow older, they must assume more responsibility for their lives—their diabetes management included. However, there is also a need and place for parental supervision. Like many adolescent conflicts, this one has no easy answer, but plenty of communication—plus the advice of a medical or family counseling professional—can lead you and your parents to a good understanding and help balance your relationship.

WILL DIABETES AFFECT YOUR RELATIONSHIPS?

The answer is a resounding no. There is no evidence that diabetics have fewer or less-fulfilling friendships than nondiabetics. In fact, a recent study in the United Kingdom looked at how children with diabetes felt about their relationships with family and friends. Although parents were often found to be a bit anxious, relationships with brothers and sisters tended to be positive. As for friends? The study found that relationships with friends were good too.[2]

On the other hand, sometimes you might be slacking on your regimen, eating things you shouldn't, not testing yourself often enough, or otherwise being careless about the management of your condition. In this case, your family and close friends would be wrong not to speak up. You'll need to really examine your behavior to know whether there is truth in what they're saying. Of course, being vigilant about your diabetes management is the best way to make sure they never have cause for concern.

As with most aspects of your social relations, communication is key. Be open and honest with your friends, and you're real friends will accept you exactly as you are. Make sure your family and friends know how you feel and clearly explain how they can help. And don't forget to listen in return!

Your friends might be uncomfortable when you first start testing your blood sugar around them. Let them know you're okay and answer their questions.

HEALTHY FRIENDSHIPS EQUALS FRIENDSHIPS FOR HEALTH

Good friends are also good for you. Studies have shown that diabetics with positive relationships with their peers tend to be psychologically healthier and also take care of themselves better and have better glucose control.

ASK YOURSELF THIS

• *How do you feel about letting other people know you have diabetes? How do you decide who to tell and who not to tell?*

• *Have you ever had any problems with treating yourself in public? What happened? What did you do?*

• *Do social situations (such as parties or meeting new people) make you nervous or uncomfortable? How much of this do you think is related to diabetes?*

• *Do you think most people are understanding about what you go through, or are they insensitive? What's been your experience?*

• *How do your family members deal with you having diabetes? Does it ever cause conflicts? How do you deal with them?*

*Your true friends will not care that you have diabetes.
In fact, they will support you as much as they can.*

I CAN'T DO THIS: RESOURCES AND SUPPORT

Brian came home from school, switched on his computer, and checked his e-mail. To his surprise, 12 messages were waiting for him. "Welcome!" read one subject line. "I go through the same thing," read another. "Re: your problem," went yet another. He always considered himself very independent, but he had to admit that sometimes managing his life with diabetes was too much to handle alone. Of course, he could always call someone on his health-care team if he had any pressing health or medical problems, but more often than not, the issues were not 9-1-1 material. Sometimes he just wanted advice about handling certain situations or tips and recommendations regarding certain products (or even just where to find them). He needed someone to turn to when erratic glucose readings drove him to frustration, when he felt lonely and separated from his peers, or when the stupid questions other kids asked about his diabetes made him angry.

On his last visit to the clinic, Brian's doctor gave him a list of online resources he could look into. He figured he might as well give it a shot and registered for one of the forums. He couldn't believe all the advice, support, and helpful links that poured in.

Besides racking up online friends and bookmarking a bunch of helpful sites, Brian learned about community groups in his neighborhood where he could meet his fellow diabetics in person.

Pretty soon, Brian started responding to other posts he saw, like "D's got me down in the

WORLD DIABETES DAY

Taking place on November 14, World Diabetes Day was created in 1991 by the International Diabetes Federation and the World Health Organization. It became an official United Nations Day in 2007. It is celebrated worldwide with events, workshops, competitions, screenings, and much more. In 2010, President Barack Obama signed a proclamation declaring all of November to be National Diabetes Month in the United States.

dumps," or "Anybody else have trouble with contact lenses?" when he thought he had something to say. He was careful not to give medical advice (the moderators were pretty good about making sure that unqualified people didn't do that), but he felt he had gotten so much from others that he wanted to give back.

So when one of Brian's new diabetic friends asked whether he'd go join an upcoming Walk for a Cure fund-raiser, Brian responded, "Where do I sign up?"

COPING

When you're first diagnosed with diabetes—and probably for a while after that—you'll likely experience a wide range of emotions, including sadness, anger, frustration, and possibly grief. As you learn about your condition and the ways to manage it, you will start coping better. Still, sometimes you'll want more information

You can talk to a parent or another trusted adult when you're overwhelmed and need support.

and reassurance that you're not alone. That's where extra resources and support groups help

If you want to step away from the computer, you can find more resources at your local library or bookstore.

tremendously. You can find detailed information about the latest diabetes treatment methods and what products and services are available.

The downside, of course, is that the Internet exists without any oversight and anyone can create a Web site and offer information and advice, whether they are qualified to do so or not. The tricky part, then, is separating the reliable from the unreliable sources.

A good place to point your mouse would be to the sites of reputable diabetes organizations or recognized medical establishments, such as the American Diabetes Association, Juvenile Diabetes Research Foundation, and Mayo Clinic. They are treasure troves of helpful, valuable, and current information. From there, you can find links to an ever-expanding world of assistance. Just make sure the information you find is geared toward the type of diabetes you have.

You can join one of the many diabetes forums, full of diabetics like yourself, parents of diabetics, and others involved in diabetes

WHO'S BEHIND THAT WEB SITE?

It's natural to go to the Internet to check out recommendations and reviews for products that you're considering. Be aware, however, that companies whose products are being recommended might be secretively running the sites. So make sure you're getting independent advice. If you're unsure, ask around. The online diabetic community is pretty tuned in, and it won't take you long to sort out the real advice from the cleverly disguised commercials.

Before taking any advice from a Web site, check to make sure it is credible.

care. And don't forget social media. There, too, you'll find dozens of diabetic groups to join, as well as individual diabetics you can "friend" and stay in contact with all the time. These resources can give fantastic support when you feel like you're the only one who has to deal with the problems you face or when you just want to vent to a group of people who will understand. Just remember: only a health-care practitioner can dispense medical advice. Some qualified health-care professionals moderate online forums, but many forums may not have a medical professional's input. Be wary of advice you get, and always check with your doctor before changing your treatment.

So, does knowing all this make you feel good? What might make you feel even better is to start giving back, as Brian did. Through local groups, online forums, and your social media network, you can find plenty of others who are newer to and less experienced with

DIABETES CAMP

Diabetes camps are a great way to meet other diabetics, learn about disease management, and have a great time all at once. Not only will you spend your summer in an environment created for your needs, but also studies have found that attending these camps have benefits that last long after the summer is over. These include better sugar control, more knowledge, a better attitude, more motivation, and higher confidence in tackling the challenges of diabetes. There are more than 100 diabetes camps across the United States and a handful more in Canada and around the world. Once you're old enough, you could be a camp counselor at a diabetes camp and help others too.

diabetes. And while you're not qualified to give out medical advice, you can share your experiences, how you managed a period of "morning high" glucose levels, or the way you handled a camp counselor who wouldn't let you go on hikes with the rest of the kids. And sometimes, just like you, others are looking for somebody to assure them that they're not alone.

ASK YOURSELF THIS

- *What do you think is your most valuable resource in coping with your diabetes? Why do you think this?*

- *What kind of resources (Web sites, books, facilities, etc.) do you wish existed but don't? How are the current resources lacking?*

- *How important are online or in-person support groups in helping you manage your care?*

DIABETES APPS

The new information frontier fits in the palm of your hand. Software applications, or apps, for smartphones and tablets are being developed for just about every purpose, and diabetics haven't been left out. Many popular apps allow you to manage your diabetes by helping you keep track of your insulin use, glucose test results, food intake, level of exercise, and many other factors. Other apps give you full nutritional information on thousands of foods so you can easily keep track on the go.

- *What have you done to help others with their diabetes care? Do you think you can do more? If so, what would that be?*

- *If you didn't have the Internet, how different do you think your situation would be?*

"Nearly every day I hear from someone like me who says that I make them feel it's okay to have diabetes. . . . I know I'm lucky because I have a family that encourages me a lot. I want to give that same inspiration to other kids with diabetes."[1]

—*Nick Jonas, of the Jonas Brothers, diagnosed with type 1 diabetes in 2005*

LOOKING TO THE FUTURE

Dressed in her cap and gown, Beatrisa stood alongside her classmates on the auditorium stage. She could barely believe she was finally graduating. *What a four years it had been!* She had been diagnosed with diabetes in her freshman year and had to

Having diabetes won't stop you from reaching your goals and having a bright future.

manage her disease through tenth, eleventh, and twelfth grades while also keeping her place as a violinist in the school orchestra.

The principal spoke to the students and the audience about "the challenges that lie ahead," and for Beatrisa, these words had special meaning. Moving into the adult world meant unfamiliar responsibilities for diabetics like her above what others would have to deal with. There would be living with roommates, possibly starting a family, and who knows what else? Likely, dozens of other issues would come up that Beatrisa never had to think about as a teen living with her parents.

Luckily, Beatrisa felt that her parents, her friends, her health-care team, and her online

HAVING CHILDREN

Many girls worry that being diagnosed with diabetes means they won't be able to have children one day. While pregnancy can make managing blood sugar levels difficult (insulin needs go down in early pregnancy and increase in later pregnancy), with proper medical care, diabetic women can and do give birth to healthy babies. The important thing is to plan ahead for pregnancy and keep blood sugars under good control before and during a pregnancy. Women should use an effective birth control method to avoid unplanned pregnancy. Breastfeeding is possible, too, though blood sugar levels will drop. The chance of your baby becoming diabetic is small, but watching for symptoms is always a good idea.

DIABETIC FIRST CLASS

In 2000, Sergeant First Class Mark Thompson received news that could have ended his short army career—he was suffering from type 1 diabetes. With the help of information from the American Diabetes Association, he was able to not only manage his disease under difficult circumstances, but he also convinced the army medical board to allow him to remain in the military. He even went on to serve in Iraq. Thompson is now a role model, showing other diabetics what they can accomplish with careful disease management and a lot of determination.

network had prepared her for this day and beyond. Over the years, she'd been given more and more responsibility for her own care. Sure, she'd be facing a transition to a new health-care team, new friends, and certainly a new lifestyle, but she was even younger and less experienced when she had to deal with being diagnosed. If she could handle that, she figured, she was ready for whatever came next.

She had already been accepted to a great college and planned to study biology. "If no one finds a cure by the time I get my degree then I'll have to discover it myself," she told her guidance counselor. Nothing was going to stop her from achieving her goal. As the principal called the students one-by-one to come forward, Beatrisa was already imagining herself in a lab when she heard her own name announced.

"Beatrisa Alarcón," the principal said over the speaker. Beatrisa proudly stepped up to shake the principal's hand and receive her diploma, her eyes staring confidently toward the future.

MORE RESPONSIBILITIES

For a diabetic, high school can be hard, but college and adulthood will be even harder. You'll be living by yourself, supporting yourself, taking on more responsibilities, and so much more. The good thing is you've already learned the basics of managing your health—now you're ready to move on to the next level.

What lies ahead? Well, you'll likely be moving out of a pediatric care and school-based health service and taking on a whole new set of

"College is a time to meet new people, experience life, and explore new possibilities, and there is no reason why diabetes should get in the way! Although managing blood sugars can be challenging while in college, staying healthy will enable you to succeed in school and to experience everything that college has to offer. The main difference between high school and college is that in college you manage the disease for yourself and you need to find your own motivation outside of your parents. The College Diabetes Network was founded for these reasons, and provides the information, connections, support, and opportunity to meet new people that help to make this transition easier."[1]

—*Christina Roth, 21, founder of College Diabetes Network*

Keep a journal or some other record now so you can refer to how you managed and coped with your diabetes later when you're on your own.

health-care providers. And remember, because diabetes complications tend to be the result of cumulative processes—that is, small effects that slowly and steadily grow until they blossom into big problems—your risk for developing them will increase. Obviously, you cannot let up on your diabetes management.

Does this mean you need to fear the future? Absolutely not! But you should start preparing for it. That means having a thorough understanding of diabetes and how to manage the disease. More than just following the instructions of your health-care team, you will have to start understanding why you're being told to make the recommended changes. This will help you when it comes time to make your own decisions about your health care. It means creating healthy habits now so you'll be able to sustain them into adulthood. The skills and techniques you develop now for handling stress, social situations, and other lifestyle choices creates a foundation that you're going to build upon later.

In adulthood, you'll definitely be facing situations you've never encountered before. If you've been though driver's ed, you

DRIVING WHILE LOW

One of the most dangerous times to experience an unexpected blood sugar low is while driving a car. Testing, and perhaps even eating a snack, right before getting behind the wheel should be as automatic as fastening your safety belt. A medical alert bracelet should always be worn while driving, since police officers might confuse hypoglycemia with being intoxicated—the symptoms can be similar. You can also get a key chain that has a small compartment to store glucose tablets.

might already be familiar with the special care diabetics have to take before they get behind the wheel. The danger of slipping out of control due to an unexpected "low" is very real. If you're female, at some point in your life you might have to deal with pregnancy and nursing. As you can probably imagine, it will affect your blood sugar management. You'll be making adult decisions about drinking and smoking, but you need to know what the added risks are with diabetes, not just the risks the rest of the population deals with. Diabetes can be an issue at work or if you want to join some kind of organization, such as the military or the peace corps.

The trick is—just like it was when you were first diagnosed—not to get overwhelmed and

CAFFEINE, CIGARETTES, AND ALCOHOL

Caffeine. The effects of caffeine and coffee in type 1 diabetics are not conclusive and the American Diabetic Association has no recommendation one way or the other. There is some evidence, however, that caffeine can reduce nighttime hypoglycemia.

Smoking. Do you really need more reasons not to smoke? Smoking is associated with the increased probability of developing conditions diabetics are at risk for. Nicotine causes veins and arteries to harden and interfere with circulation. This can only make complications such as heart disease, stroke, kidney disease, nerve damage, foot problems, and many others worse. This risk is under your control. So don't smoke.

Alcohol. Alcohol can interfere with glucose metabolism and lower your blood sugar both right after you drink and up to 8 to 12 hours later.

*Managing your diabetes is a lifelong task,
but future technological and scientific
advancements might make the process easier.*

to seek support when you are. With every day
that passes, more and more information is
discovered to help diabetics with their struggles.
Every day, better medications, more discreet
and precise devices, and more helpful resources
become available. And somewhere, the elusive
cure awaits.

Meanwhile, thanks to the efforts of many
people and organizations, there's more
awareness of diabetes among the public and

less discrimination. There's no reason for that trend not to continue. The support you've built up won't be affected just because you've moved away. Your parents and your closest friends, too, are never more than a phone call away. And no matter what new problems you confront, plenty of diabetics have faced the same or worse, and come out on top.

ASK YOURSELF THIS

- *Do you have any fears about the future and your diabetes? What are they? What can you do to alleviate them or address them?*

- *What do you most look forward to? Do you foresee having diabetes as affecting that in any way? If so, how will you deal with that?*

THE SEARCH FOR A CURE

Currently there is no recognized cure for type 1 diabetes, but that doesn't mean this will be true in the future. A lot of time, money, and effort are going toward finding a cure, and a breakthrough might not be far away. The Juvenile Diabetes Research Foundation (JDRF) outlines two main areas that show particular promise: immune therapies and beta cell therapies. Immune therapies are aimed at preventing the immune system from destroying the body's insulin-producing beta cells without affecting your ability to fight off other diseases. Beta cell therapies refer to restoring islet beta cells in the body, so insulin production can occur naturally.

- *Has having diabetes prepared you more for adulthood? If so, in what ways?*

- *Do you feel you've adequately prepared yourself for the challenges ahead? What do you think you could do to be even more prepared?*

- *Has diabetes changed the way you look at your long-term goals? How?*

JUST THE FACTS

Insulin is a hormone that allows sugar in the blood to pass through cell membranes and provide energy to the body.

Type 1 diabetes is an autoimmune disease wherein the immune system attacks and destroys the insulin-producing cells in the pancreas.

Type 2 diabetes is a condition in which your body can produce insulin, but it either does not make enough or the body doesn't know how to use the insulin once it is released.

Constant thirst and the urge to urinate are the primary symptoms of diabetes. Other symptoms include weight loss, hunger, fatigue, and numbness and tingling of the extremities.

While there seems to be a genetic risk factor for developing type 1 diabetes, there is no known cause of the disease.

If left untreated, diabetes can be fatal.

There is no cure for diabetes, but administering careful doses of insulin effectively manages the condition. This is combined with careful testing of blood sugar.

Insulin can be administered by syringe injection, insulin pen, or electronic pump.

The most common hazard to diabetics is low blood sugar, or hypoglycemia, which can be reversed by ingesting a fast-acting sugar.

Diabetics are at higher risk for a wide variety of conditions affecting almost every area of their bodies.

Diabetics should pay attention to their diet, particularly when it comes to identifying carbohydrates and counteracting their effects with insulin.

With proper management, type 1 diabetics can eat almost anything, including sugar, that nondiabetics can.

Exercise is particularly important for diabetics because it is an effective tool for lowering and maintaining steady blood sugar levels.

It's essential that other people be aware of your condition in case of an emergency. At the very least, a medical alert bracelet should be worn.

Many resources are available both online and in most communities, providing diabetics with information and support.

As one gets older, particularly when diabetics transition from pediatric to adult care, new challenges arise. Education in diabetes management is an ongoing process.

WHERE TO TURN

If You Sense Low Blood Sugar

Good job on being in tune with your body. You'll want to test your blood sugar immediately. If it's low, consume a small amount of something containing glucose as soon as you can. It's a good idea to keep glucose tablets, sugar packets, or juice boxes handy so you will have something to grab when you start to experience low blood sugar. You want to take action before your blood sugar falls too low. In that case, you could pass out and would need a friend, family member, or medical professional to inject synthetic glucagon directly into your bloodstream. Remember, it's always best to be aware and act before the situation becomes an emergency.

If You're Getting Teased

Unfortunately, bullying is a common occurrence and happens often in schools and anywhere else kids get together. No one deserves to be made fun of—not for looks, brains, or medical conditions. If someone is giving you a hard time for testing your blood or wearing a monitor on your hip, tell that person to stop. If the harassment continues, talk to a teacher or school counselor for additional advice and help with the problem.

If You Have Any Problems or Issues

Luckily, help shouldn't be too far away. For critical medical questions, seek the advice of your health-care team or other qualified medical professional. For smaller issues, ask your family and friends for help. If you want to get advice from the diabetic community, help is as close as the nearest computer. There are numerous creditable online resources out there, with information, advice, and forums filled with diabetics like yourself who are happy to discuss different aspects of living with the disease and can lend a virtual "ear" when you feel overwhelmed or just want to vent.

If Someone You Know Has Diabetes Symptoms

Someone you know is constantly thirsty and urinating much more than is normal. You're right to be concerned. It's important that you recommend that person to contact a medical professional as soon as possible and tell him or her why. If the situation becomes an emergency and he or she is unable to do it, you need to call for medical help immediately. Do not try to diagnose or treat this person yourself, as there could be a different medical issue happening. Only a doctor using a variety of blood sugar tests can make a definitive diagnosis. The more symptoms a person exhibits in addition to hunger and thirst, the more likely they are to be further along in the disease and the more critical it is to get treatment.

GLOSSARY

basal insulin
Insulin taken for baseline control of blood sugars.

blood sugar level
The amount of glucose dissolved in the blood; also known as blood glucose level.

bolus insulin
Insulin taken to counteract a person's meal or high blood sugar.

carbohydrates
Sugars, starches, and other foods that provide energy for the body in the form of sugar.

glucagon
A hormone produced by the pancreas that raises blood sugar levels. It is injected to counteract extreme hypoglycemia.

glucose
Often used interchangeably with "sugar," it refers to a specific molecule of carbon, hydrogen, and oxygen, which is easily broken down by the nondiabetic body to release energy.

hypoglycemia
Abnormally low blood sugar.

immune system
The system in the body that fights off diseases by attacking the agents that cause them.

insulin
A hormone secreted by the pancreas that regulates blood sugar and allows glucose to be converted into energy.

insulin reaction
Abnormal lowering of blood sugar due to an excess of insulin.

islet beta cells
The cells in the pancreas responsible for producing insulin.

ketones
Acids produced when the body burns fat rather than glucose for energy.

pancreas
A small, spongy gland behind the stomach that secretes digestive enzymes and hormones, including insulin.

trigger
Something that initiates a process or reaction.

type 1 diabetes
An autoimmune disease in which the immune system destroys the insulin-producing cells of the pancreas, making the body unable to regulate blood sugar levels on its own.

type 2 diabetes
A disorder in which insulin can be produced, but the pancreas does not produce enough or the body cannot use it effectively.

ADDITIONAL RESOURCES

SELECTED BIBLIOGRAPHY

American Diabetes Association. American Diabetes
Association, 2011. Web.

Diabetes Monitor. DiabetesMonitor.com, 2011. Web.

Endocrineweb. Vertical Health, 2011. Web.

Juvenile Diabetes Research Foundation International.
Juvenile Diabetes Research Foundation International,
2011. Web.

*U.S. National Library of Medicine National Institutes of
Health.* U.S. National Library of Medicine, 2011. Web.

FURTHER READINGS

Hanas, Ragnar, and Stuart Brink. *Type 1 Diabetes: A Guide
for Children, Adolescents, Young Adults—and Their
Caregivers.* New York: Marlowe, 2005. Print.

Hood, Korey K. *Type 1 Teens: A Guide to Managing Your Life
with Diabetes.* Washington DC: Magination, 2010. Print.

Loy, Spike Nasmyth, and Bo Nasmyth Loy. *Getting a Grip on
Diabetes: Quick Tips and Techniques for Kids and Teens.*
Alexandria, VA: American Diabetes Association, 2007.
Print.

Moran, Katherine J. *Diabetes: The Ultimate Teen Guide.*
Lanham, MD: Scarecrow, 2004. Print.

WEB LINKS

To learn more about living with diabetes, visit ABDO Publishing Company online at **www.abdopublishing.com**. Web sites about living with diabetes are featured on our Book Links page. These links are routinely monitored and updated to provide the most current information available

SOURCE NOTES

CHAPTER 1. WHAT'S GOING ON WITH ME? DEFINING DIABETES

1. Susan Brink. "Obesity Problems Fuel Rapid Surge Of Type 2 Diabetes Among Children." *Kaiser Health News*. Henry J. Kaiser Family Foundation, 21 Mar. 2011. Web. 25 May 2011.

2. "Diabetes Statistics." *American Diabetes Association.* American Diabetes Association, n.d. Web. 25 May 2011.

3. Ibid.

4. "Fact Sheets: Type 1 Diabetes Facts." *Juvenile Diabetes Research Foundation International*. Juvenile Diabetes Research Foundation International, Dec. 2010. Web. 25 May 2011.

5. Ibid.

6. Sarah Wild, et. al. "Global Prevalence of Diabetes: Estimates for the Year 2000 and Projections for 2030." *Diabetes Care* 27. 5 (2004): 1047–1053. PDF file. 25 May 2011.

CHAPTER 2. WHY ME? CAUSES AND RISK FACTORS

1. "A Decade of Progress in Diabetes Research." *USCF*. University of California San Francisco, 24 Sept. 2010. Video. 25 May 2011.

2. "Diabetes—Type 1—Causes." *University of Maryland Medical Center*. University of Maryland Medical Center, n.d. Web. 25 May 2011.

CHAPTER 3. BEING RESPONSIBLE: TREATMENT AND MANAGEMENT

1. "Fact Sheets: Type 1 Diabetes Facts." *Juvenile Diabetes Research Foundation International*. Juvenile Diabetes Research Foundation International, Dec. 2010. Web. 25 May 2011.

CHAPTER 4. IT'S ALL ABOUT THE FOOD: DIET AND NUTRITION

1. Danielle Hembree. Personal interview. 5 Jan. 2011.

SOURCE NOTES CONTINUED

CHAPTER 5. LIVING ON THE EDGE: POTENTIAL COMPLICATIONS

1. Anna Caro. Personal interview. 24 Dec. 2010.
2. Grace Shih. "Diabulimia: What It Is and How To Treat It." *Diabetes Health*. Diabetes Health, 3 Mar. 2009. Web. 25 May 2011.

CHAPTER 6. ADJUSTMENTS HERE AND THERE: A NEW LIFESTYLE

1. Joel Melara. Personal interview. 16 Jan. 2011.

CHAPTER 7. FRIENDS, SCHOOL, AND INSULIN: DEALING WITH SOCIAL ISSUES

1. Kaylene Mangum. Personal interview. 17 Jan. 2011.
2. RC Povey, et al. "Children's Beliefs about the Impact of Their Type 1 Diabetes on Their Family and Peers: An Exploratory Study." *Practical Diabetes International* 22. 9 (2005): 333–338. Web. 25 May 2011.

CHAPTER 8. I CAN'T DO THIS: RESOURCES AND SUPPORT

1. Debra Manzella. "Nick Jonas and Bayer Diabetes Care Join Forces for Kids with Type 1 Diabetes." *About.com*. About.com, 7 Aug. 2008. Web. 25 May 2011.

CHAPTER 9. LOOKING TO THE FUTURE

1. Christina Roth. Personal interview. 25 Jan. 2011.

INDEX

ABOUT THE AUTHOR

MK Ehrman is a freelance writer and editor. He has written numerous magazine articles and self-help books for children, teens, and adults.

PHOTO CREDITS